MW00826895

The Art and Practice of Modern Flute Technique

VOLUME ONE

BY

WILLIAM KINCAID

IN COLLABORATION WITH

CLAIRE POLIN

© 1967 (Renewed 1995) Universal - MCA Music Publishing, Inc., a Division of Universal Studios, Inc.
All Rights Reserved
No portion of this text may be reproduced without the express written consent of the Publisher

PREFACE

TO THE TEACHER:

It is the sincere hope of the authors that *THE ART AND PRACTICE OF MODERN FLUTE TECHNIQUE*, projected through several volumes, will provide a practical and valuable guide to the flute from which the student will begin the study of his instrument and expand his knowledge and technique to the point of sufficient proficiency for normal performance purposes. One generally finds that the average child is sufficiently developed in manual dexterity and reading comprehension to be able to begin study of the flute by about age nine or ten, although younger students have been known to make some progress. The first volume of this method, while applicable to any student, is directed chiefly to the beginner who has already mastered some of the rudiments of music and is able, therefore, physically and mentally to devote himself to learning the techniques of the instrument itself.

Wherever necessary, the teacher should expand upon an area of learning by using additional materials to help the student master each new idea thoroughly before proceeding onward. The larger sections of learning are here called "lessons," although it is recognized that some of these will consume several lesson hours, while others may be absorbed more rapidly, depending upon the individual student's abilities and needs.

The authors wish to thank the following for their kind cooperation in preparing this volume:

Miss Sonoko Mimura, for valuable assistance in copying.

Staff of the Elkan-Vogel Music Company.

Mrs. Katherine B. Walder, for valuable assistance with the reproduction of materials.

Mr. Lawrence Fritz, for photographic work.

Mr. Hans Moennig, for permitting photographic reproduction of his piccolo.

WILLIAM MORRIS KINCAID was born on April 26, 1895, in Minneapolis, Minnesota. He began the study of the flute at the age of seven in Honolulu, where his father, a Presbyterian minister, had accepted a pastorate. The youngest of four children in a very musical family, young William also studied the piano at an early age, but was discovered to be spending more of his time diving for coins and shells off the pleasant beaches of Hawaii than in practicing music indoors. However, when he noticed an old flute (evidentally a family heirloom), lying around the house, his interest was awakened. After hearing a concert of the Royal Hawaiian Band, he began to practice quite seriously. Subsequently, his piano study and underwater swimming were to play an important part in his musical development and in his extraordinary breath control on the flute.

Upon the family's return to the United States to a new pastorate in Charlotte, North Carolina, the boy demonstrated that he was on the road to mastering another instrument, for at his father's urging, he had learned to play the organ in church. The flute, however, was soon to become his central interest. He made such remarkable progress that by the time he entered Columbia University as an undergraduate, he was allowed to study simultaneously with the renowned master, Georges Barrère, at the Juilliard School of Music, from which he subsequently graduated.

Two years in the Navy briefly interrupted, but did not retard, his promising career. He soon became recognized as a distinguished flutist in his own right, joining the New York Symphony and the Chamber Music Society (a group made up of first-chair men in Walter Damrosch's orchestra), and touring the country. Shortly thereafter, he began collecting rare and unusual flutes from the Orient and other parts of the world (see *Figure D*).

In 1921, at the invitation of Leopold Stokowski, Kincaid accepted the position of solo flutist with the Philadelphia Orchestra, a post he held with world-wide acclaim for forty years, and with which group he appeared as soloist at least 150 times. Kincaid has been the recipient of many distinguished honors. He has received honorary doctorates from the Curtis Institute of Music, Temple University, and Combs College of Music, all in Philadelphia. He has been the recipient of the much-coveted Medal of Achievement of the Philadelphia Art Alliance, and the Kuhn Award for distinguished musicianship, given annually by the Philadelphia Orchestra.

William Kincaid has performed throughout the world and his name is an international byword for fine flute playing. Today, he continues to teach, at the Curtis Institute and privately, those chosen few who are privileged to study with him, and who, in some cases, are willing to commute transcontinentally in order to seek him out. It is no exaggeration to say that most of the younger generation flutists of note today are Kincaid products.

His recordings are unfortunately all too few and have become collectors' items.

Concerto in G by Mozart (Columbia)

Brandenburg Concerto No. 5 by Bach (Columbia)

Award Artist Recordings (2 discs) (Columbia)

Music for the Flute (flute & piano) (Columbia)

Poem by Griffes (flute & orchestra) (Columbia)

Suite in A Minor by Telemann (RCA)

Claire Polin has been actively associated with William Kincaid for several years, both as a student and, currently, as a successful flute teacher of the Kincaid technique. Her education included study at Temple University, the Juilliard School of Music, and the Philadelphia Conservatory of Music, where she received a doctorate in musicology. She is the author of *Music of the Ancient Near East* (Vantage Press) and has written innumerable articles for scholarly journals. She is active both as a concert performer and as a composer. Dr. Polin is on the Faculty of Rutgers University and Director of the University Exchange Concerts locally for the People-to-People Committee of Washington, D. C.

Acknowledgements

We wish to thank the following for permission to reprint excerpts from the works quoted:

CONCORDIA PUBLISHING HOUSE, St. Louis, Mo.,
for: *A Little Shepherd Music* by H. Rohlig

SOCIÉTÉ Des ÉDITIONS PHILIPPO, Paris,
for: *Sicilienne* by Fusté-Lambézat
Sérénité by Passani

DEDICATED TO THE MEMORY OF MY WIFE, HELEN KINCAID,
WHO ENCOURAGED THIS EFFORT

LESSON I

INTRODUCING THE FLUTE

Figure A

A Brief History of the Flute

The flute is one of the oldest instruments in man's recorded history, mentioned in the Bible and in other literatures of antiquity. By Beethoven's day, many variants of the Western flute existed, including the flageolet (played horizontally without keys) and the recorder (played vertically). Although Quantz, himself a fine flutist, did much to improve the instrument, it was not truly playable until the great teacher-flutist, Theobald Boehm, scientifically reconstructed the instrument in 1850 into its present form. Boehm acoustically rearranged the tone-holes and finger-keys so that the instrument became less cumbersome to manipulate. Simultaneously, the intonation became truer and the tone more brilliant.

The flute has had many famous admirers, among whom were some of Europe's royalty. From Pan in Greece to Confucius in China, from Leonardo da Vinci in Italy to Czar Nicholas II in Russia, the flute has retained its popularity with both professionals as well as amateurs. Several of the composers mentioned in this volume were both famous performers on the flute as well as composers for it. Drouet, for example, was first flutist for the King of France, while Kummer retained a similar position in the court of the Duke of Saxe-Coburg. Quantz was first court flutist as well as teacher of the heir-apparent to the throne of Prussia. The latter in due time became Frederick the Great, performer and composer of flute music who, we are told, almost wept the day he ascended the throne because it meant less time with his beloved flute.

Flutes have been made of many different materials, from the simple reeds in ancient times to the lavishly gem-studded one of Drouet, or the glass-and-pearl flute with silver keys played by Joseph Bonaparte. Until this century, most flutes were made of ebony wood, frequently with an ivory head-joint (see *Figure B*). However, since metal flutes are capable of stronger tone, it has become customary to play silver ones, although some of solid gold or platinum are available and produce an excellent tone.

Figure B

The family of flutes commonly used in this century is shown below. They are, from lowest pitch to highest (from top to bottom):

ALTO FLUTE IN G

FLUTE IN C (OPEN-HOLED WITH B KEY ADDED)
    (sometimes called French model)

FLUTE IN C

PICCOLO

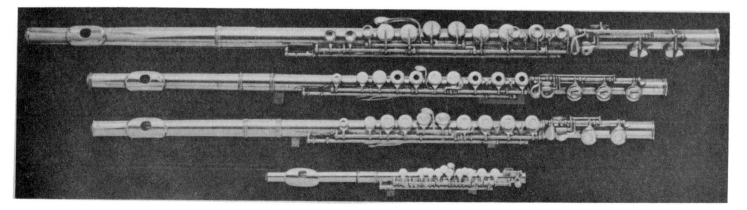

Figure C

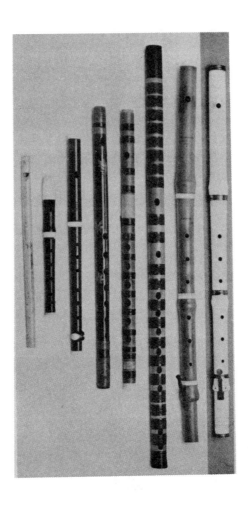

Figure D

From the Kincaid collection of rare and Oriental flutes

Right to left: ivory flute made in England and given to Mr. Kincaid by Leopold Stokowski; a brown wood replica of the one-key Boehm flute; two bound bamboo Chinese flutes; Japanese lacquer flute brought back by Efrem Zimbalist; single-key ebony and ivory piccolo; piccolo 4-note recorder; knuckle-flute made by Powell.

For further information on the flute, the student is directed to the following books:

My Story of the Flute by L. De Lorenzo (Citadel, N. Y., 1951)

Bibliography of the Flute by Dayton Miller (Cleveland, 1935)

Music of the Ancient Near East by C. Polin (Vantage Press, N. Y., 1954)

The Flute and Flute-Playing by T. Boehm, Transl. by D. Miller (Dover, N. Y.)

Music of the Most Ancient Nations by C. Engel (London, 1864)

The Story of the Flute by H. Fitzgibbon (Reeves, London, 1928)

Music of the Bible by J. Stainer (Novello, London, 1914)

PARTS OF THE FLUTE

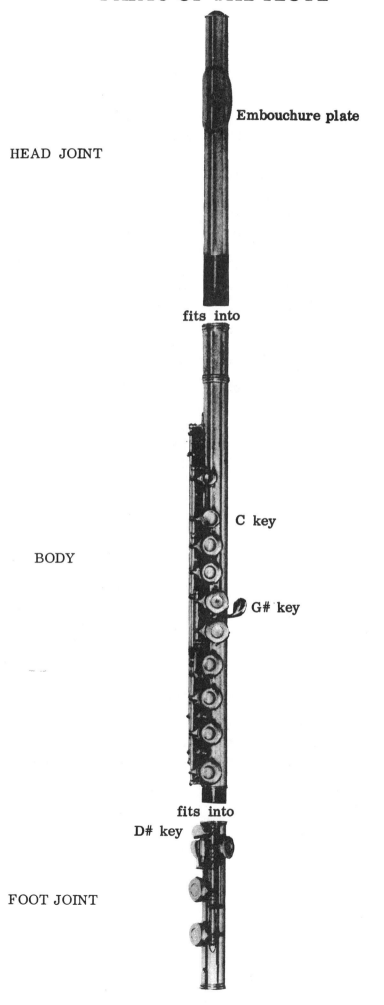

Embouchure plate

HEAD JOINT

fits into

BODY

C key

G# key

fits into

D# key

FOOT JOINT

Figure E

HOW TO HOLD THE FLUTE

Figure F

HAND POSITION

Looking down on your own hands as you hold the flute:

Figure G

Thumb position of the flute:

Figure H

Figure H1

How someone else looks to you as he holds the flute:

Figure I

Notice the points of contact:

LIP PUSHES AGAINST THE FLUTE

LEFT HAND PUSHES *IN* AGAINST THE FLUTE

RIGHT HAND PUSHES *OUT* AGAINST THE FLUTE

These form the

First Triangle, or tripod, of *position*, thus:

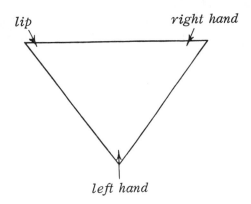

TO THE STUDENT:

THE CARE OF YOUR FLUTE

The flute is a valuable instrument and you will be able to enjoy playing it for a long time with a minimum of repairs if you handle it carefully and with respect. Your teacher should check your instrument's condition periodically. It would be wise to follow these rules:

1. Keep your flute clean at all times. INSIDE, it should be cleaned with a soft piece of cloth threaded through your rod and gently inserted into each section. OUTSIDE, you should carefully wipe off all finger and lip marks *after each use* with a dry, clean cloth. Avoid silver polish, waxes, and rough cleaning cloths if you wish to keep your flute looking new. If, after some time, you notice that the pin areas are becoming dusty, you should *very carefully* dust these with a pipe-cleaner or cotton swab. Should any of the pins come loose, your teacher can probably replace them immediately.

2. Place your flute, when not in immediate use, on a flat surface or table with the keys facing upward, never downward. Always keep your flute in its case overnight or after practicing.

3. Avoid sudden movement with your flute in order to eliminate costly dents, etc. Should you notice a cork, pad or pin missing, tell your teacher or take it to a reliable repairman. Do not attempt to repair it yourself.

LESSON II

PRODUCING TONE

Before trying to produce a tone on your instrument, try the following exercise. Get a small, empty, narrow-necked bottle and blow *across* the opening to produce "whistle sounds." Next, blow *into* it, but at an angle to get a "full-tone sound." Notice how different your lips "feel" when they produce first the "whistle" then the "full" sound. This shift in lip position is referred to as the <u>embouchure</u> and will make possible the production of all the tones on the instrument. Repeat this several times to learn how to shift the embouchure from one quality of sound to another. You will discover that the larger the bottle, the deeper the tone. When producing the "full" sound on the bottle, try to blow for a long time, holding the tone like a fog-horn.

Now you are ready to try the same procedure on the flute. To produce a tone, take the <u>head</u> <u>joint</u> of the flute out of the case (*Figure E*), set the <u>embouchure</u> <u>plate</u> under your lower lip, partly covering the hole but leaving it sufficiently open to produce sound. Blow at an angle until a clear tone is produced. Note that the tip of the head joint is to your left, the open end to your right. Your lips cover only the *edge* of the hole.

Next, try again and blow harder as you form the tone. Pinch your lips as if you were about to whistle. You will probably hear the same note an octave *higher*. Now, cover the open end of the head joint with your right palm. You should hear the octave *lower*. It is advisable to experiment a bit with producing the higher and lower tones easily. It is very beneficial in establishing a clear concept of the difference in lip positions, or embouchure.

Let us try something else now. Blow ever so slightly with relaxed lips on your embouchure plate – gently, just as you blew on the empty bottle. This may produce far-off whispery tones, similar to bag-pipes. Close the end of the flute with your palm, and blow just at the level of a whisper. These sounds are called <u>overtones</u> or <u>harmonics</u>. Overtones enrich and give character to TONE. Any given note can be made to produce overtones; by overblowing, even the twelfth and the octave above are easily reached. This is sometimes called the "scale of nature," produced solely by overblowing, without changing the fingering at all. The overtones you have played are based on A for your head joint alone, but were you to assemble your flute completely and play the overtones on the lowest note, C, they would sound approximately like this:

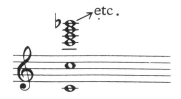

Try this on A, using the head joint again, and see how many you can hear as distinctly different pitches.

The Bagpipe Exercise

Produce *low* whistle tones

Pinch your lips, blow across for upper sounds ↗

Relax lips, blow down for lower sounds ⤵

Repeat slowly

If we slow down the overtones and blow more firmly, we can produce the same sounds as TONE.

We are now ready to learn how to shape our lips and produce the

Second Triangle of *lip position*

(embouchure) for *clear tone*, thus:

Smile slightly.
Purse lips a trifle, bringing the center of the lips *forward* on the embouchure plate to act as fat cushions upon which the air will travel. To help the tone, jut out your jaw a bit. Pretend to look like a fish in the aquarium. Form this triangle of lip muscles:

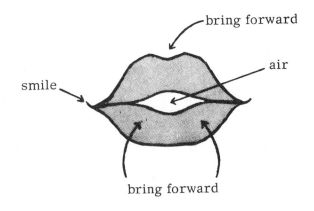

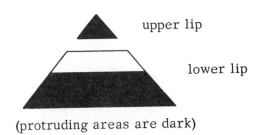

(protruding areas are dark)

SHAPING THE LIPS FOR THE EMBOUCHURE

It is important for the student to learn the proper <u>attack</u> with the very first notes he learns to play. Using only the head joint, smile, purse your lips to form the proper position on the embouchure plate, place *tongue* between the lips. Pretend that something is on the end of your tongue and spit as if saying *Too* to produce tone. We call this a <u>spitato</u> attack. Now, try this again and hold the tone as long as you can *Toooooooo*. Next, try the same procedure closing the end of the flute. What you are doing is called "attack" or "articulation." The term <u>articulation</u> applies to the way you tongue the notes (spitato or otherwise), or fail to tongue them by <u>slurring</u> (fingering different notes without moving your tongue).

Here is a helpful exercise in *attack.*

Say: *tee   tah   toe.*

Now, shape your lips for the attack embouchure and say rhythmically:

        tee   tah   toe - - - - tee   tah   toe.

Be sure the tongue is between the lips at the start of each "t"; in other words, "spitato."

Try to sing Tee-Tah-Toe to the tune of *Three Blind Mice.*   Tongue your breath as you would sing.

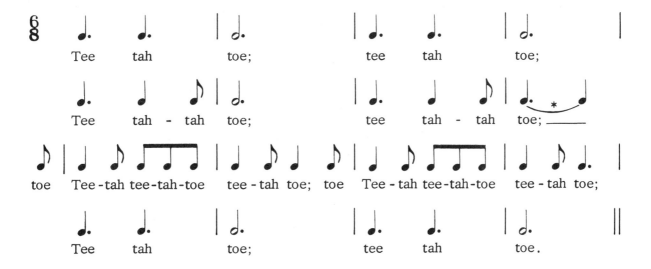

*This curved line is a "tie." It connects notes on the same pitch and signifies that they are to be played as one continuous tone, without tonguing the second note.

CHART A

LOW AND MIDDLE REGISTER FINGERINGS

SECTION I : SCALE OF C MAJOR

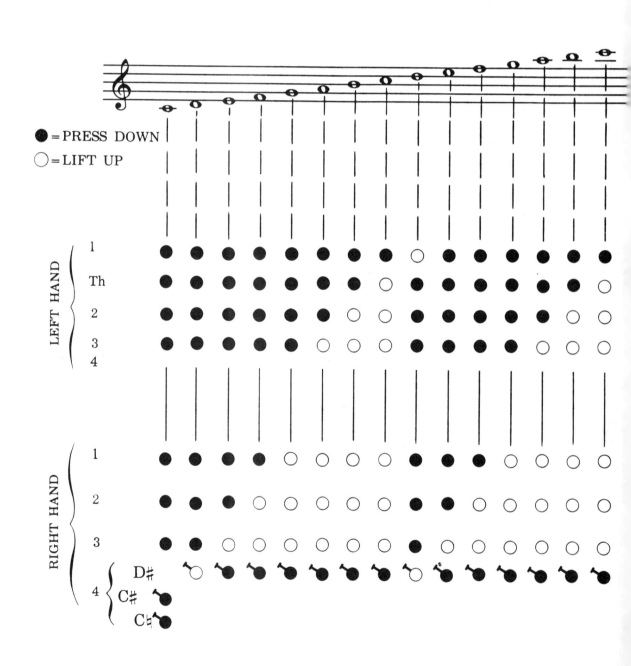

NOTE: thumb and four fingers are counted, not five fingers.

SECTION II : CHROMATIC FINGERINGS

also possible —
preferred —

	1	2	3a	3b	4	5a	5b	6	7	8	9	10	11	12
LEFT HAND 1	●	●	●	●	●	●	● ⚷★	○	○	●	●	●	● ⚷★	○
Th	●	●	●	●	●	●	⚷★	○	●	●	●	●	⚷★	○
2	●	●	●	●	●	○	○	○	●	●	●	○	○	○
3	●	●	●	●	●	○	○	○	●	●	●	○	○	○
4														

	1	2	3a	3b	4	5a	5b	6	7	8	9	10	11	12
RIGHT HAND 1	●	●	○	○	○	●	○	●	○	○	●	○		
2	●	●	○	●	○	○	○	●	○	○	○	○		
3	●	●	●	○	○	○	○	●	●	○	○	○		
4 { D♯	⚷	⚷ ⚷	⚷	⚷ ⚷	⚷	⚷	⚷	⚷	⚷ ⚷	⚷ ⚷				
C♯	⚷													

★ ⚷ B♭ key

CHART B

NOTE AND REST VALUES

a	Whole-note	𝅝	or	Whole-rest	▬	equals
2	Half-notes	𝅗𝅥	or	Half-rests	▬	each of which equals
2	Quarter-notes	♩	or	Quarter-rests	𝄽	''
2	Eighth-notes	♪	or	Eighth-rests	𝄾	''
2	Sixteenth-notes	𝅘𝅥𝅯	or	Sixteenth-rests	𝄿	''
2	Thirty-second-notes	𝅘𝅥𝅰	or	Thirty-second-rests	𝅀	''
2	Sixty-fourth-notes	𝅘𝅥𝅱	or	Sixty-fourth-rests	𝅁	

Note: Very rarely an even faster indication, a hundred-twenty-eighth-note 𝅘𝅥𝅲 may be found in music

A dot after a note extends its duration by one-half.

METER SIGNATURES

indicate the *type* and *number* of beats to the measure:

$\dfrac{4}{4}$ ←how many? = $\dfrac{4}{♩}$ $\dfrac{2}{4}$ = $\dfrac{2}{♩}$ $\dfrac{3}{4}$ = $\dfrac{3}{♩}$ $\dfrac{5}{4}$ = $\dfrac{5}{♩}$
   ←what kind?

$\dfrac{4}{2}$ = $\dfrac{4}{𝅗𝅥}$ $\dfrac{3}{2}$ = $\dfrac{3}{𝅗𝅥}$ $\dfrac{2}{2}$ = $\dfrac{2}{𝅗𝅥}$ $\dfrac{6}{8}$ = $\dfrac{6}{♪}$ $\dfrac{3}{8}$ = $\dfrac{3}{♪}$

$\dfrac{7}{8}$ = $\dfrac{7}{♪}$ $\dfrac{9}{8}$ = $\dfrac{9}{♪}$ $\dfrac{12}{8}$ = $\dfrac{12}{♪}$ etc.

C is an abbreviation for $\dfrac{4}{4}$

¢ (called *alla breve*) is played twice as fast as **C** and counted like $\dfrac{2}{2}$: ♩ ♩ ♩ ♩

EXERCISES IN MUSICAL RHYTHMS

Tap out the following rhythms over and over again until they become easy for you. Before playing a new piece or exercise, tap out the rhythm *first*

Example A: Quarter-note values

Example B: Eighth-note values

Example C: Mixed rhythms for the rhythmically advanced student

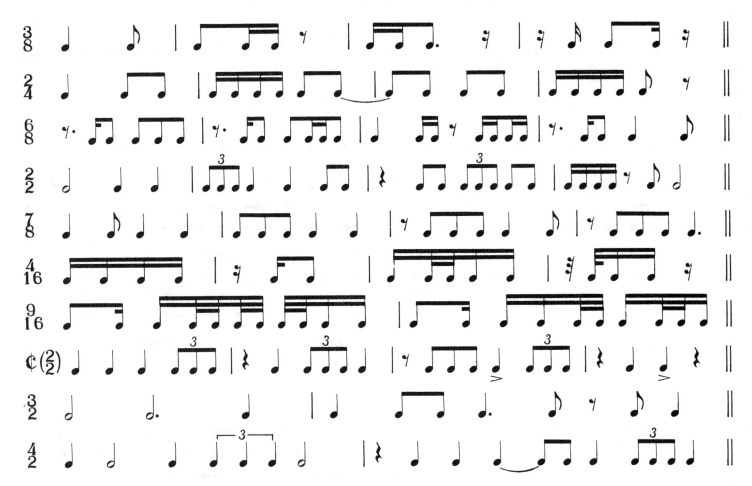

Exercise D: How to count in some simple tunes:

First, sing each song through once. Then hum it again and tap out each note. Finally, count the beats while tapping each note. (Note: if your teacher prefers that you count with "ands," be sure to do so throughout each beat of the piece and not just occasionally.)

TEN LITTLE INDIANS

Allegro (fast)

POP! GOES THE WEASEL

(* Since 6 here is an "upbeat," it is borrowed from the last measure.)

CHART C
USEFUL TERMINOLOGY AND DYNAMICS

Dynamic Markings:

pp (pianissimo) - very soft

p (piano)   - soft

mp (mezzo piano) - medium soft

mf (mezzo forte) - medium loud

f (forte)   ˙ - loud

ff (fortissimo)   - very loud

sf, sfz (sforzando) - accent, within the indicated dynamic level

rf, rfz (rinsforzando) - heavy accent, within the indicated dynamic level

$>$ - accent mark, single note stressed within the indicated dynamic level

cresc., ⟍⟍ (crescendo) - getting louder gradually

dim., ⟍⟍ (diminuendo)- getting softer gradually

decresc. (decrescendo) - getting softer gradually

⌒ (fermata) - hold as long as you like

:‖ - repeat exactly entire section

D. C. (Da Capo) - return to the beginning

D. S. (Dal Segno) - return to the sign 𝄋

Fine - the end

⌐1.⌐ :‖2.⌐ ‖ repeat indication to go back and play all until the second ending,
then play that instead of the first ending.

sempre - always, or continue in the same way

subito - suddenly

Common tempo indications:

Prestissimo - fast as possible
Presto   - very fast
Vivace   - lively
Allegro   - fast
Allegretto - somewhat fast
Moderato - moderate speed
Andante   - comfortably slow; strolling tempo
Andantino - somewhat slow
Lento   - quite slow
Adagio   - slow and stately
Largo   - very slow and heavy
Grave   - slowest possible
rit. (ritardando) - slowing down gradually
rall. (rallentando) - slowing down
accel. (accelerando)- getting faster gradually

Common mood indications:

cantabile   - singing
leggiero   - lightly
pesante   - heavily
marcato   - accentuated
espressivo - expressively
dolce   - sweetly

LESSON III
ADDING FINGERINGS

Review your head joint exercises and have your teacher show you how to assemble your flute. Be sure to align it as shown in Chart A. Refer to the illustration of the proper position (*Fig. F*). Hold the end of your flute up almost horizontally. Look into a mirror and be sure that you look like this:

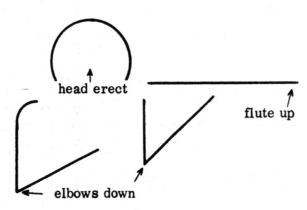

Remember your *triangles* of position and embouchure.

Holding your flute firmly, take the fingering for Middle D (refer to Chart A) and blow firmly but do not force the tone. Try to hold the tone *Toooooooooo* as long as possible without squeaking or buzzing or getting flatter. Help yourself by recalling the bottle exercise. These fingers are down:

Left Hand: thumb, 2, 3
Right Hand: 1, 2, 3

Refer to *Figure F* for the D position as played.
Also to *Figure G* for your thumb placement.

Here is the note you are playing:

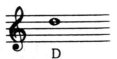

D

We have started with this Middle D on the flute in order to teach you the correct position for this note which is often played incorrectly, and start you off with most of your fingers on the flute. You will thus gain confidence, for all you have to do, in most cases, is to *lift* off one or more fingers to produce other tones.

Next, *add* only R.H. 4 on the Eb key. Now you are able to play

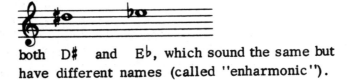

both D♯ and Eb, which sound the same but have different names (called "enharmonic").

Follow these directions and you will add more tones:

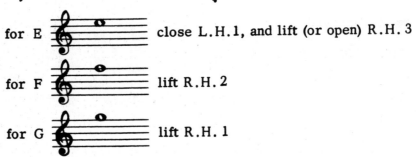

for E   close L.H.1, and lift (or open) R.H. 3

for F   lift R.H. 2

for G   lift R.H. 1

As you go, you will improve your tone if you blow a tiny bit harder at first and blow *across* the flute rather than into it. Reverse this and blow downwards when going *down* to a lower tone.

Remember that whenever you play, all parts of you must coordinate. Music starts with your *brain* and works its way down to the *lips* (embouchure), *tongue* (articulation), *chest* (breathing), and *fingers*— all of which must function simultaneously.

Try the following exercises. Sustain the sound of the long tones by blowing *continually*, while counting the beats mentally. Take a quick breath wherever ❯ appears. Naturally, always breathe on a rest.

Try each of the following exercises slowly until the fingers move from position to position automatically. Some notes are harder to move between than others because "sloppy" extra sounds are likely to creep in; for example, from D to E, or D♯ to E, etc. Play very precisely, moving the fingers down or up *simultaneously*. Then, play the same thing a bit faster. For variety, change the rhythm of all the exercises you play. This will avoid monotony, and at the same time, enable fingers and mind to practice the same materials in many different ways. Students who employ their imagination always enjoy practicing because it becomes a creative challenge instead of the drudgery of mere repetition.

Thus, Exercise 5 could be practiced in long-short rhythm:

or in reverse rhythm:

Exercise 8 could be played in any of these rhythms:

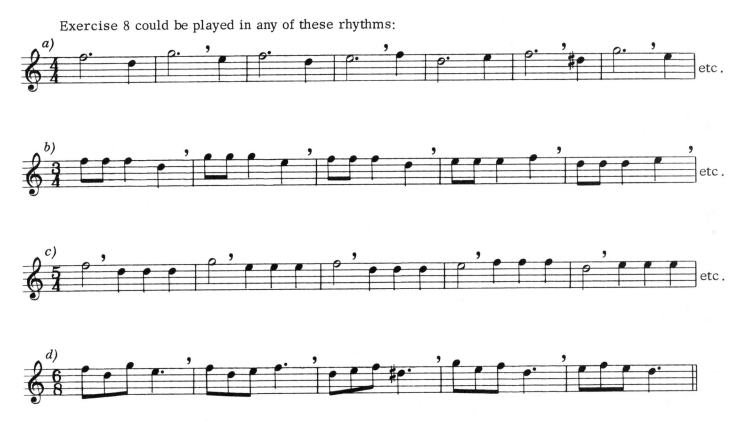

Create a new rhythm for the above if you can.

9. Variations on Simple Phrases

When you have become more dextrous and can change fingers rapidly, try these brief exercises and duets.

18.

EASTERN MELODY
(Duet)

19.

TRUMPET TUNE
(Duet)

20.

AU CLAIR DE LA LUNE
(Duet)

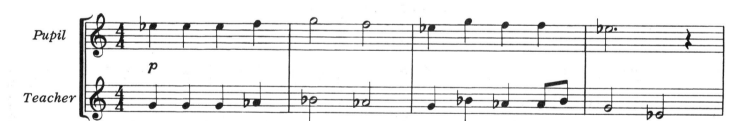

LESSON IV
UP AND DOWN

Let us add some new fingerings. If you refer to Chart A for the fingering for F♯ (same as G♭), you will be able to play the following exercises.

1.

Observe skips in intervals and rhythms.

2.

In the following, notice breaths after the long notes only.

3.

OLD LULLABY
(Duet)

In the above, it is advisable to try two measures at a time. Be sure your TONE is clear and firm. Your teacher will help you to become aware of "in-tuneness." First, learn your fingerings, then tap out the rhythm,

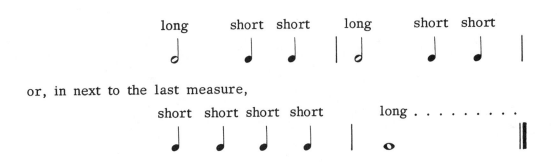

or, in next to the last measure,

Let us try this duet with different rhythm, long - - - - - short - short:

WALTZ

*Remember F♯ is still good! An accidental remains unchanged throughout the measure.

The next one is slightly more difficult. Count most carefully! Your teacher can prepare you to achieve the feeling of the *short -long - - - - - short* beat which is called syncopation.

JAZZ

DOTTED NOTE STUDY

GAY DANCE

11.

12.

13.

14.

15.

DUO

Pupil

Teacher

16.

Pupil

Teacher

NEW TONES going down: change the direction of your wind (breath) and you will discover that it is possible to produce the same notes an octave lower with the same fingering, thus:

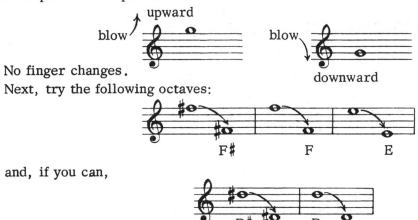

No finger changes.

Next, try the following octaves:

and, if you can,

Remember, on *low D* and *low D♯* we add L.H. 1.

After tonguing each note, try the octave paired and slurred, that is, *tongue* the first note but not the second (or others) covered by the *slur*

Change direction of wind and add L.H. 1,
but do not *attack* the low note.

When this is mastered, try these exercises with octaves. Push hard on the quick notes to get the octave to sound. Arrows show the direction of the wind, so think "up" or "down" accordingly.

16. "I'm Tricky" Play slowly and *count*.

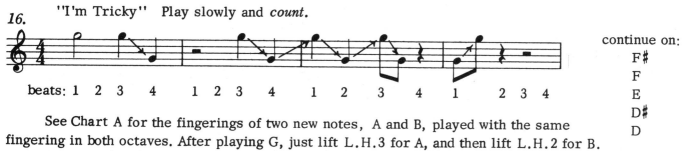

beats: 1 2 3 4 1 2 3 4 1 2 3 4 1 2 3 4

continue on:
F♯
F
E
D♯
D

See Chart A for the fingerings of two new notes, A and B, played with the same fingering in both octaves. After playing G, just lift L.H.3 for A, and then lift L.H.2 for B.

In the following exercise, watch the rests carefully. Be careful to finger all notes correctly. For variety, play all of it backwards, keeping the same notes and meter:

17.

A SAD TUNE

Here are some familiar tunes. Review the dotted note rhythms and tap out the melodies first to check your rhythm. Afterwards, play these an octave lower.

18.

MARY HAD A LITTLE LAMB

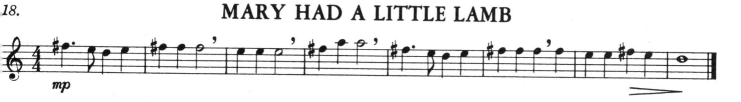

BRINGING IN THE SHEAVES
(Old Hymn)

Prepare this one by tapping with a pencil:

long   short long   short long

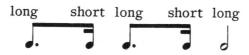

Then, practice from B to D in order to get the transition smooth.

(Tongue)

B

Moderato

Review both pieces, this time with <u>dynamics</u> (loud and soft markings). Refer to Chart C.

Part of the pleasure of playing music is to play with other people. The next piece is a "round" and can give you a great feeling of accomplishment by playing it not only alone but with others. Here are the rules: Player Number One starts at the beginning where marked. When he reaches the measure marked ②, Player Two starts at the beginning while Player One continues. When Player One arrives at ③, Player Three starts at the beginning while the others continue. Therefore, the first Player ends earliest, the second next, the third last. Meanwhile, listen to your own part and do not become confused by the other parts. This form of abbreviation of what we call in music a "canon" or "round" was invented in the Middle Ages.

FRÈRE JACQUES

Just to be sure that you understood the rules, here is the solution to the abbreviated form, or what it sounds like played together:

1.

FOLK TUNE

2.

PETITE DUO

3.

LIGHTLY ROW

4.

REPEAT TUNE

5.

ECHO SONG

TUNES OLD AND NEW

1.

TEN LITTLE INDIANS

2.

TWINKLE

3.

GAY TUNE

4.

HOP, SKIP, JUMP!

5.

WINDING

(now with slurs)

6.

WALTZ OF THE SKIPS

7.

DUET FOR COUNTING

after T. Benoît-Berbiguier

LESSON V

FILLING OUT THE OCTAVE

Just one more note and we shall be able to play two complete octaves. Look at Chart **A** for the fingering for Middle C: You will note that this is played like B except that the thumb is lifted off. By now you have learned that most fingerings on the flute are an orderly matter of starting with all keys down and *lifting* one by one as you go up. To reverse your direction, start with one finger position, C, and add fingers in the proper order to go down. Lowest C: is played exactly like low D♯, but slide R.H. 4 over the roller or farthest key (we refer to this as the C Natural Key). Thus, C one octave above Middle C is fingered like Middle C but overblown, like most octaves. If you feel insecure on the C's, rest your left hand thumb on a small knob you will find next to the B keys. Do not be afraid of dropping the flute; you will not if you observe the "pull" and "push" suggestions in the *First Triangle of position.*

In order to "warm up" and aid in developing smooth fingering, most musicians practice scales the first thing each day. Begin with a C Major Scale. Tongue each note and hold it as long as you can.

The low C is difficult to sound, but try it.

Next, try the G Major Scale.

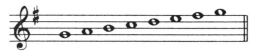

Now, try each scale again and make each note begin *forte* and become *piano* (See Chart **C**), or the reverse, *piano* and then *forte*. Then a pair of notes, p ——— f; f ——— p. Thus, daily exercises would be something like this:

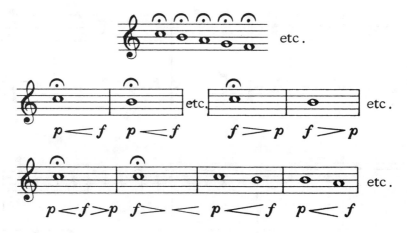

or, possibly with many other variations, using all the notes you are able to play. Make up your own exercises, too. Be sure to practice with *slurs* as well as *attacks*.

WHOLE- AND HALF-NOTES
DUET FOR INTONATION*

Exercise 1:

Allegro

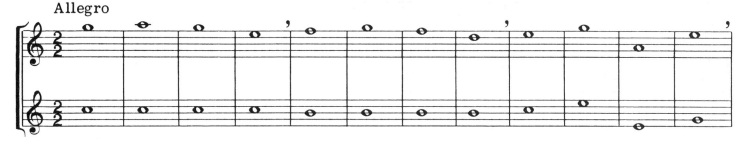

In the following exercise some tied notes appear. Two notes on the *same* line or space on the staff can be tied together: Sound the first note and hold it for the *added* length of time of the second note. Thus, = or three beats.

HALF-, QUARTER- AND TIED-NOTE DUET

(With clues as to how to play each one)

Exercise 2:

mp "I am even."

(*Intonation is "in-tuneness"; listen to yourself as you play.)

b) "Marching"

c) "Late start"

*tie

d) "Wait for me!"

DUET ON DOTTED AND EIGHTH-NOTES

Exercise 3:

Each note should be *attacked* clearly. No speed is indicated, so you may practice this piece as fast as you can play it well.

VARIATIONS ON A THEME

DUET FOR MIXED NOTES AND SLURS

Exercise 4:

MIXED RHYTHMS

Exercise 5:

(Note that at each number a new rhythm is introduced. Tap out the rhythms first, then play the notes.)

EIGHTH-NOTE DUO

Exercise 6:

EASY SOLOS (To Achieve Dexterity)

Watch the dynamics in order to make the music more graceful. When in doubt, refer to Chart C.

ON TOP OF OLD SMOKY

LAVENDER'S BLUE

THE KERRY DANCE

THEME FROM THE NINTH SYMPHONY
(Duet)

Beethoven

DUETS FOR TONGUING AND EVEN TEMPO

▾ = heavy *tu*, slightly explosive on the "t". *Exercise 2* is a study in syncopation. The secret lies in moving from the short to the long note quickly and in counting. Note that at X both parts are syncopated, while at Y the upper part is syncopated against the steady rhythm of the lower part.

1.

Allegro

2.

Allegro

EASY PIECES

1. YANKEE DOODLE

2. SONG

J. Blow

3. CANTABILE

R. Schumann

4.

RAINDROP WALTZ

(Emphasize the melody notes.)

The dots over the notes mean ''staccato,'' or to be played *short* but not *fast*.

5.

THE MUFFIN MAN

In the following, note the dot over the *end* note of a slur. Do *not* tongue this but merely lighten or ''lift off.'' Thus, the D in measure 2 is slurred too, but shortened.

6.

MENUET FROM BACH

46

Here is your first concert piece with piano accompaniment.

Play it slowly and evenly and contrast the dynamics.

Be sure to hold the *fermata* extra long and breathe after it.

CHORALE

R. Schumann

A famous piece arranged for two flutes. You may learn both parts, although the lower has one new note. A gavotte is a rather jolly dance, so do not play it too slowly.

GAVOTTE

A. Corelli

Andantino

ADDITIONAL MUSIC SUGGESTED FOR STUDY

Any easy hymns or nursery songs

Easy Duets by Koehler (C. Fischer, New York)

Gavotte and other easy movements from the
Sonata for Three Flutes by Boismortier (Boosey & Hawkes, N.Y.)

LESSON VI
HOW AND WHAT TO PRACTICE

Scale practice is essential to being able to play almost any kind of music. Let us, therefore, add another new fingering from Chart A for C♯ (for middle and high C♯ lean the thumb on the knob). Also, if you master the fingerings for G♯ and B♭, we shall be able to play in several keys with ease. Note that the B♭ position referred to is different for the A♯ position, for while both notes sound alike, the B♭ is more practical to use in all flat scales and key signatures while the A♯ is better for sharp keys or any key involving the transition from A♯ to B natural.

SCALE WARM UPS FOR DAILY USE

(New notes are marked * .)

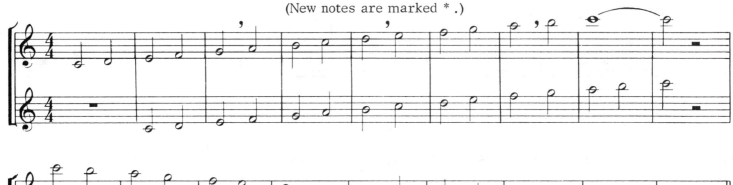

All scales except C Major have *sharps* (♯) or *flats* (♭) in them. To avoid writing these through the piece as "accidentals," the proper sharps or flats for each key are placed at the beginning of each staff. This is called a <u>key signature</u> and identifies each scale. Memorize which sharps or flats are in each scale *before* playing it. To help yourself remember, there is no harm in circling each sharp or flat lightly in your music until you are able to remember it automatically.

Thus, G Major may also be written

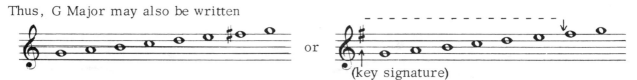

or

(key signature)

In the key signature, all F's, high and low, are sharped in this scale. * will serve as a reminder of the sharps or flats.

G Major Scale

(⊛ Second flute may start when you are here.)

D Major Scale

A Major Scale

F Major Scale

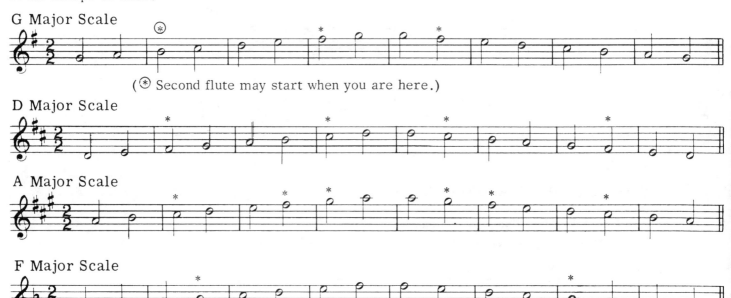

SCALE EXERCISES

The following scales should be practiced in strong rhythm daily until they can be played smoothly and fast. They may be tongued or slurred. Some are written in sixteenth-notes to accustom the student to reading fast music and playing it without hesitation.

C Major: (This is the name of the key.)

Breathe rapidly through the *mouth*. If necessary, subdivide the phrase in order to catch an extra breath until you can play faster.

G Major:

50

D Major:

* High C# fingering same as middle register.

A Major:

watch!

F Major:

BREATHING EXERCISES

You may have noticed by now that you seem to nave insufficient breath. Here are some valuable suggestions for developing and controlling your "wind" or breath.

1. Stand erect when playing, spine straight, legs about a foot or more apart. Always inhale by *mouth*, never by nose. Why take a thimbleful of air when you can have a bucketful? Open mouth (not too wide) and quickly "swallow" or gulp a deep breath. Try not to make any noise when doing this. Pretend you are a detective about to dive into a cold lake at midnight in order to catch an unsuspecting thief. Silence! Speed! *Deep* breath!

2. The Accordion Exercise: With arms on hips and with legs apart, take a *slow*, deep breath through your mouth, then slowly and forcibly breathe out until your lungs collapse. Continue 10 to 15 times, but do not allow yourself to get dizzy or too tired.

3. The Candle Exercise: Light a candle and hold it with both hands about 12 inches from your lips at the level of the collar-bone. Inhale through the mouth, shaping your lips as if you were playing the flute, and then *slowly* blow the candle until the flame *flickers*, but neither goes out nor remains still. This will develop control for long breaths.

4. Push-ups: Lie on the floor, face down, arms bent at the sides, legs together, knees stiff. Inhale deeply through the mouth and hold your breath. Slowly lift up on your hands and toes until the body arches off the floor. Hold this position until the breath is gone completely. Exhale. Repeat. Vary by inhaling, pushing up, and slowly sinking to the floor again. Push up and sink 4 to 6 times in *one* breath. Gradually increase the number of push-ups by daily practice.

5. Pull-backs: For a quick vertical push-up, do the following. Take normal standing position, legs apart. Lift arms over head, elbows straight. Inhale and hold breath. Pull arms down hard at your sides, elbows bent. Try to touch your waist with your elbows by arching your back as if to bring your elbows together at the back. Exhale and relax.

Now, when trying scales in the following pattern, see how much easier it is to hold your breath. First, tongue each note, then slur every other measure, where eighth-notes appear. Play all other scales similarly.

The following are presented as examples of clear articulation (tonguing) and smooth fingering.
Apply breathing rules.

PETITE DUET

Here is another very attractive solo with piano accompaniment.
Always tune first to the piano. (Your teacher will demonstrate).

HYMN

Ch. W. Gluck

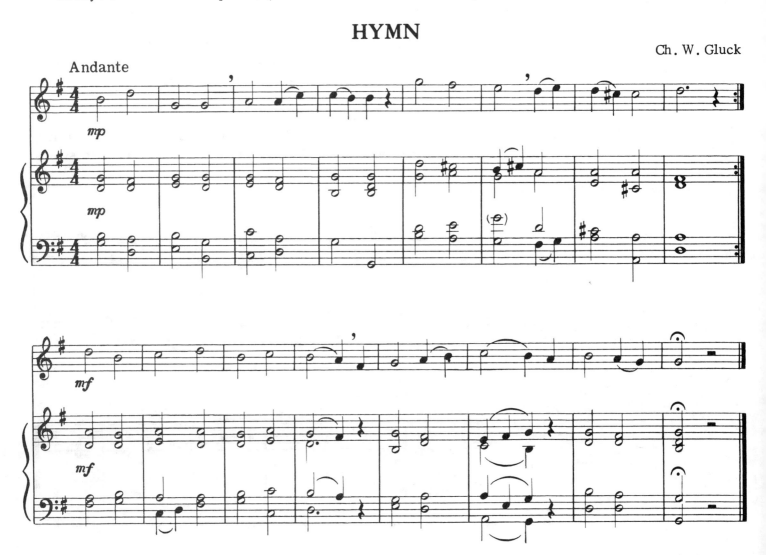

THE CHROMATIC SCALE

If you were to play each half-step possible in alphabetical order, you would be playing a scale called "chromatic." The same effect can be achieved by starting on any note. Here are some short rhythm-and-note studies using the chromatic scale. Some notes sound the same but have *two different names*; these are called "enharmonic" notes and the fingerings are marked to help you.

*(use A♯ here, B♭ coming down)

*(same as D♯)   *(same as C♯),

←rhythm→

*(same as G♯)   *(same as F♯)

Write your own chromatic exercise beginning or ending on any note.

3. (The rhythm is important.)

SLOW-MOTION BUMBLEBEES   (The brackets show directional phrasing.)

4. a)

b)

c)

VARIATIONS ON A THEME: WAYS TO PRACTICE

ADDITIONAL SCALES

E Major:

(new #)

(arpeggio or broken chord)

(Articulate 4 different ways.)

B Major:

(various articulations)

Arpeggios

In the following exercise, note that an additional articulation is introduced: semi-tonguing. Here is a list of the most frequently seen articulations and how to play them:

1) *no marking*: tongue "ta" or "da" depending on speed desired.

2) *staccato*: short "ta"

3) *semi-tongued*: softly elided *dd* as in "Daddy"

4) *slurred*: tongue first note of the slur.

5) stress firmly, say "dah"

6) shorter stress, "tah", like emphatic staccato

MIXED NOTES AND ARTICULATION STUDY

G. Boehm

Andantino

EXERCISES FOR FINGER DEXTERITY

1. Allegro

Play the above exercise also one octave *lower*. Also try tonguing throughout.

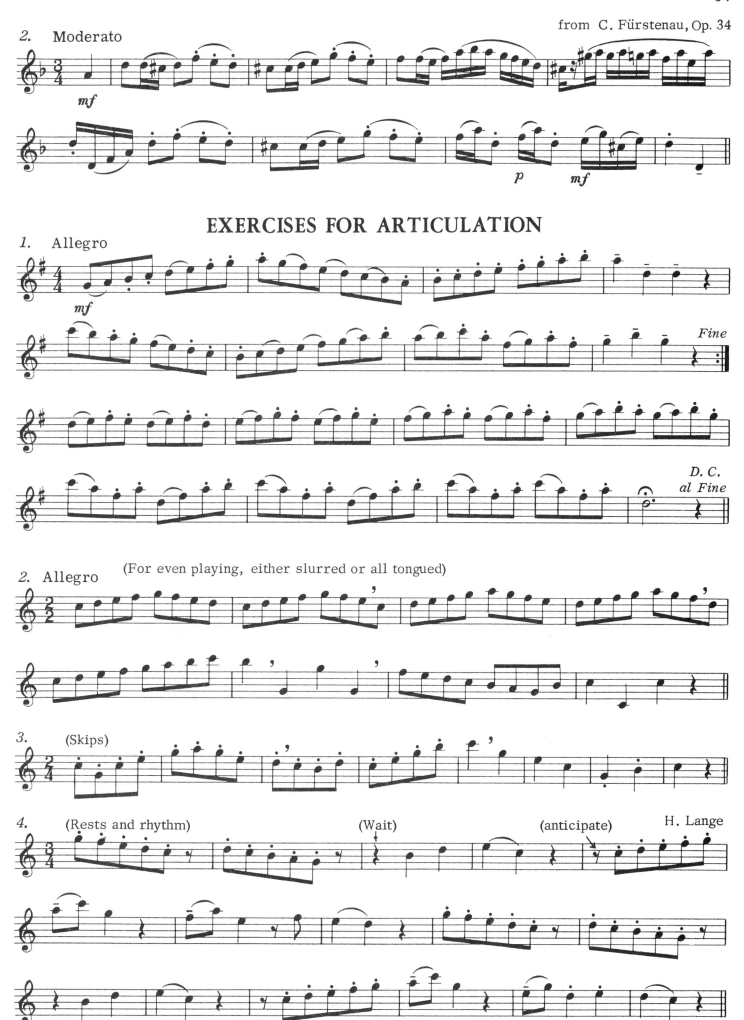

EXERCISES FOR ARTICULATION

SOLOS FOR ARTICULATION

(Suggestion: Review the scale of each piece first.)

MENUET

T. Hotteterre

1.

mf (p 2nd time)

LONDON BRIDGE

2.

Now, play this in C Major, reading one note higher.

DUO

from E. Koehler

Allegro

The following has two problems:

1) the staccato must be *exactly* together,
2) unisons must be *perfectly* in tune.

SOLDIER'S MARCH

R. Schumann

EXCERPTS FOR FLUTE AND CELLO

N. Strungk

MENUET
Moderato

Now we introduce two versions of the same piece, a *Sarabande* by Lully. Version A is arranged for flute and piano, version B for flute and any bass instrument, such as bassoon or cello.

When playing with piano, remember that this is an "untunable" instrument, unlike the flute or violin. Therefore you must adjust your tone to it. First, play low A, then A one octave higher, and compare these notes with the same ones on the piano. Your teacher will help you to adjust your intonation (in-tuneness).

When repeating a section of a piece, make the music more interesting by playing it a bit differently; for instance, if the first time it should be *mf*, play it *mp* the second time, or vice versa. Note also the construction of the piece. The phrase lengths in this one are varied, first three bars, then four bars. Be sure to emphasize this by breathing in the correct places.

SARABANDE

(Version A)

J. B. Lully

SARABANDE

(Version B for flute and bassoon, or any other bass instrument)

64

Here is a piece by a contemporary composer which utilizes the low register in a lyrical manner. Practice each phrase in different octaves to control tone quality and fingering. Note that there is no meter signature, so count each equivalent of a quarter-note as one beat and wait momentarily at the broken bar-line, as one does in a hymn. Most of the first theme feels in $\frac{4}{4}$ or $\frac{8}{4}$. Where the "German carol" is indicated, play approximately twice as fast so as to avoid dragging the longer notes. This section feels in three, more or less. One can then learn the entire piece, which has an interesting organ part not included here. The flute articulation is suggested in place of all tonguing, but it may be changed if desired.

A LITTLE SHEPHERD MUSIC

H. Rohlig

Copyright 1958, Concordia Publishing House, St. Louis, Missouri
Reprinted by permission.

AIR VARIÉ

T. L. Tulou

EXAMINATION I

It is time now for a general review of everything learned thus far. The following ten exercises will test your accuracy and knowledge of key signatures, dynamics, meter signatures - all of which should be inspected carefully *before* playing.

ADDITIONAL MUSIC SUGGESTED FOR STUDY:

Solos: *Lied,* by Wurmser (Editions Philippo, Paris)
Song of a Chinese Fisherman, by Maganini (Musicus, New York)

Collections: *La Flûte Classique,* by Classens et Le Roy, Vol. I, (Combre et Cie, Paris)
Flutist's Classic Duet Repertoire (Witmark, N. Y.)

Ensembles: *Three Little Duets,* by Schubert (Mercury, N. Y.)
Little Girl Rocking Her Doll, by Rebikoff (Musicus, N. Y.)
Little Recorder Book, by V. Persichetti (Elkan-Vogel, Phila.)

LESSON VII

WHERE TO BREATHE

There are some fundamental rules with which every student should become acquainted concerning right and wrong breathing places. If the student comprehends and masters the general practice, he will need to rely upon the teacher only for special problems. Here are some basic rules:

1. If notes are of mixed values (long and short), breathe after the longest note.

Example:

2. If notes are of equal value, breathe between repeated notes.

Example:

3. If notes are of equal value and there are no repeated notes, breathe *after the first note* (or down beat) of the new measure.

Example:

4. In a continuous or flowing passage, it is well to breathe after the change in direction.

Example:

5. Generally (except in triple rhythm), *avoid* breathing on the barline.

Thus, in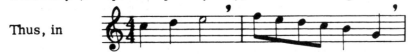

breathing is marked after the longest tone available.

But, in

breathing is in normal place.

However, in

breaths can be taken *after* the down beat as inconspicuously as possible.
Instead of thinking of the beats as

 etc.

think of the beats as going *somewhere*. Hence,

etc.

would imply that the notes are grouped so as to create a "running" or moving pattern which remains flowing with no interruption in the rhythm.

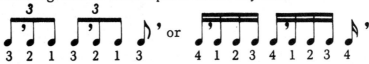

Here, one can breathe after the first note of any group in order to inflect it properly.

Notes are to music what letters are to words, spelling out meaningful sounds. Groups of notes are like *syllables* in speech. Just as syllables resolve in a feeling of punctuation, or rest, so musical syllables resolve in a feeling of down-beat upon a note or a rest. It takes at least two beats to establish the feeling of how long a beat is in music, so it is a good rule never to breathe until *after* the beat has been established.

Think of the downbeat as the ending to the previous syllable, while the second note begins the next syllable and resolves in the next measure. The rhythmic impulse can be thought of as:

Hence, it is generally safe to breathe *after* the *downbeat* in most kinds of music which "flows," or *before* the anacrusis (or upbeat).

Mark the correct breathing places in the following:

In the following exercises and pieces, try conscientiously to breathe *only* where marked. If you cannot quite make it to the nearest breath mark, breathe quickly off the nearest long note:

nearest long note

EXERCISES FOR BREATHING AND SKIPS

mf (Finger the skips firmly.)

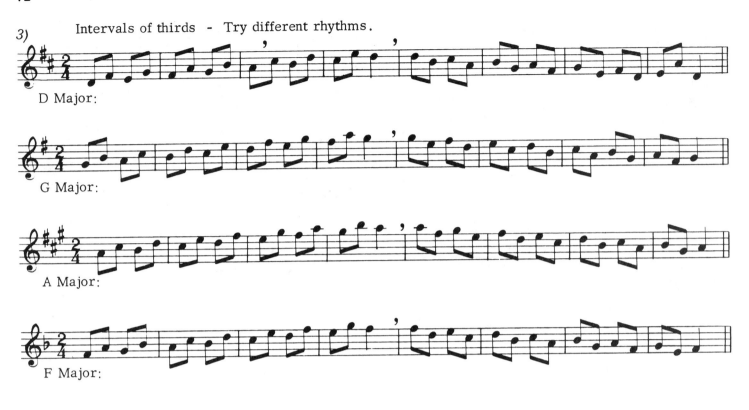

3) Intervals of thirds - Try different rhythms.

D Major:

G Major:

A Major:

F Major:

All music is made up of <u>scales</u> and <u>intervals</u>. These materials are basic to music, just as fabric and thread are basic to clothing. The common intervals are called by these names:

unison (or prime) second third fourth fifth sixth seventh octave ninth tenth

INTERVAL PRACTICE

1)

Later, add:

2) Try in all keys:

* Teacher may begin when student is here.

SCALE STUDIES TO BE PLAYED IN ALL KEYS

NEW SCALES

Bb Major:

E♭ Major:

A♭ Major:

INTERVAL EXERCISE STRESSING MELODY TONE

Allegro

f

MUSIC FOR PLEASURE
(Watch breathing.)

1.
LULLABY
J. Brahms

Slowly

2.
AMARYLLIS
Louis XIV of France

Dance like

3.
MARINES' HYMN

Lively

4.
THE ASH GROVE
Old Welsh Tune

Moderato

NOBODY KNOWS THE TROUBLE I'VE SEEN

(A good study in slow syncopation.)

Spiritual

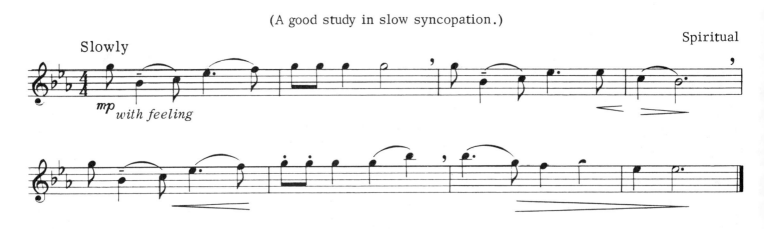

Below is an old English Christmas carol printed on two instead of four staves, as you might be likely to see it. You may play any part, but be sure that you find the part you are playing at the moment on the next staff. Roman numerals indicate parts played; Flutes I and III have stems up; Flutes II and IV, stems down.

OLD ENGLISH CAROL

For long breath, here is a fine duet to learn to play in good phrasing.

Practice both tongued and slurred.

H. Soussmann

78

In most of the following ensemble pieces for two or more flutes, the parts are interchangeable and of relatively even level of difficulty. You are advised, therefore, to learn all the parts and to apply the basic rules of phrasing and breathing to each part.

RUSSIAN CHILDREN'S SONG

arr. C. P.

In the following excerpt from Handel's *Passacaglia*, be sure to coordinate with the second flute in the "long-short" rhythm by practicing "Tah teh-Reh teh-Reh teh-Reh", etc.

G. F. Handel

ADESTE FIDELES

A SONG OF GALILEE

BOURRÉE

J. B. Lully

Allegretto

In the following, notice how the theme returns often. Breathe where marked and "color" it with dynamics.

MUSETTE

R. d'Hervelois

Allegro

SARABANDE

W. Corbett

LESSON VIII
ARTICULATIONS

The term "articulation" covers many different kinds of tonguing. Articulation "shapes" the music just like an outline shapes a picture. Therefore, we not only tongue each note, *ta-ta* or *tee-tah-toe*, but we also *slur* notes and frequently alternate tongued and slurred notes to give clearer contour (and meaning) to the music we play.

A slur looks like a *tie* but extends between notes on *different* pitches:

The first note is tongued and the others are fingered and blown, but *no tongue* is used. Keep the breath going:

Tah - - - - - - - -

Try the following exercise. Remember that *repeated notes must be tongued*; in a slurred passage only tongue the first of the slurred group:

For clear, crisp tonguing, try *tu* (not *too* but the French sound between *ee* and *oo - u*). To do this, smile, say *tee* and gradually while sustaining the sound purse lips as if to whistle or to kiss someone; this should produce the French *tu* sound. This will aid you greatly in producing rapid staccato tonguing.

Fast

Tongue this same exercise *slowly*, and instead of *tu*, say *dah*. This is called "semi-legato" tonguing and is sometimes marked ; or in slower music, Generally, however, where a dot is over a note, or the beginning of a slur is indicated, or a piece has no markings over the notes but is in a very fast tempo, it is safe to tongue *tu*. In slower tempi, or with other markings over notes, one can generally tongue *dah*. Below are some easy exercises and solos for you to train yourself to play with correct articulation.

Ex. 1

Ex. 6
Allegretto

SCALES IN MIXED ARTICULATIONS

DUO

L. Dorus

The following exercise should be practiced in *all* keys. Try it in G major, A major and B♭ major, for instance, by either visually transposing or actually writing it out for yourself in these keys. Watch the direction of the phrases. The brackets will help you to isolate the difficult parts and to practice these first as a preparatory etude.

SHORT SOLOS
(To be played with good expression and precise articulation.)

1. **Allegretto**

MENUET

N. J. Hüllmandel

Below is a piece in abbreviated form. Parts A and B are written out. To make this a true "rondo," A must always return after each new statement, so that the final form is A B A B A C (?) A etc. You may make up a C section if you like, but be sure to end with A.

2. **Moderato**

RONDO

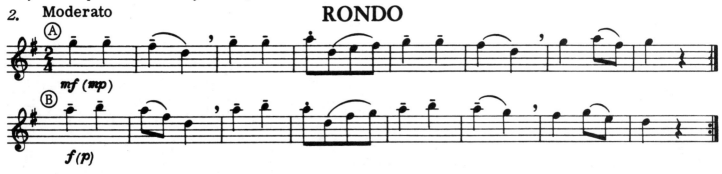

3.

MENUET
(Feel this in one beat, or impulse, to a measure.)

G. P. Telemann

4.
ECHOS
(Note the three-measure phrases which are not very commonly found. "Color" the repeats.)

Moderato

J. Hotteterre

5.
MENUET
(Note how the themes are constructed and altered or varied. This construction is called the "form" of the piece. Learning the form will help you memorize more easily.)

Moderato

J. B. Lully

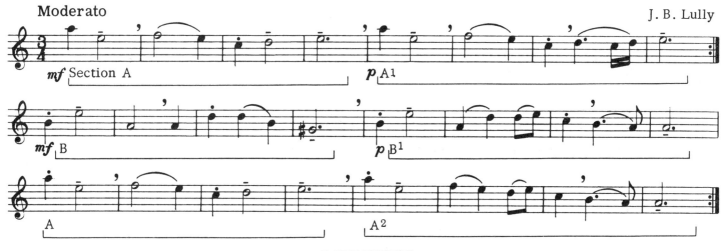

6.
MENUET
(For smoother fingering, practice slowly this part * and get a bit faster day by day. These phrases can be tongued either way, in groups of 4 and 2 notes, or in 6 notes to a slur.)

Moderato

L. Caix d'Hervelois

7.
A LITTLE SONG

Andantino

After D. Kabalevsky's
Children's Pieces, Op. 27

8.

MOVEMENT
(From a sonata)

B. Marcello

9.

PROVENÇAL SONG

(Easy notes but tricky rhythm. At *, if you "untie" this the first time, it will be easier to play.)

Note, in the next one, the varieties of articulation, consisting of:

a) staccato tonguing   c) slurred notes

b) heavy tonguing   d) semi-legato tonguing

10.

GAVOTTE from "Armide"

C. W. Gluck

Andantino

11.

MELODIE

after L. v. Beethoven

HELPFUL EXERCISES

WALKING THE DOG

1.

(Syncopation)

2.

SKATING

(Smooth sixteenth-notes)

3.

SKIPPING

(Dotted notes)

(Think ♪. ♪ so you will play the final note late enough.)
1 2 3 4

4.

FLOATING

(Smoothness)

5.

STEPPING LIGHTLY

(* Brackets are for practice units; do each individually, then join together until all are smooth.)

6.

RONDO

(Rapid tonguing)

H. Soussmann

Allegretto

GYMNASTICS FOR THE LIP

(Go slowly in these. Get faster only as the fingering becomes even. Beware of squeals in the tone. Fingering to watch: middle D♯ (open key) and E. Bracketed areas first.)

In the following, the problem of where to breathe becomes obvious immediately. It might be advisable to practice all *tongued* at first; then, all *slurred* ; finally, as marked. Each measure is a complete section. Note brackets for phrasing.

Frederick The Great

ENDURANCE TEST FOR THE TONGUE

(Break up the following etude into sections for study purposes. Emphasize the accidentals as they appear, to make them sound deliberate rather than as errors. Breathe after changing direction, and write in the breathing places yourself, but consult with your teacher to be certain that you understand the rules.)

Schneider

In the following duets, note the uneven phrase lengths characteristic of pre-classical music. "Shape" each section correctly by breathing in the proper places.

1.

ANDANTINO

J. B. Lully

Try either articulation in the following. Which, in your opinion, sounds better suited to the piece?

2.

ALLEGRO

12th - century
troubadour song

3.

RIGADOON

(Tongue lightly.)

H. Purcell

(Note: When bass-clef parts are given, they may be played by any lower-register instrument. It is not necessary to play these always as duets, but it certainly will help the student who is concerned with developing a beautiful tone and a good sense of rhythm to have someone to play with at home or at his lesson. If desired, the teacher may show the student how to transpose these bass parts up one octave so that two flutes can play the parts.)

4.

ANDANTE FOR FLUTE AND CELLO

G. P. Telemann

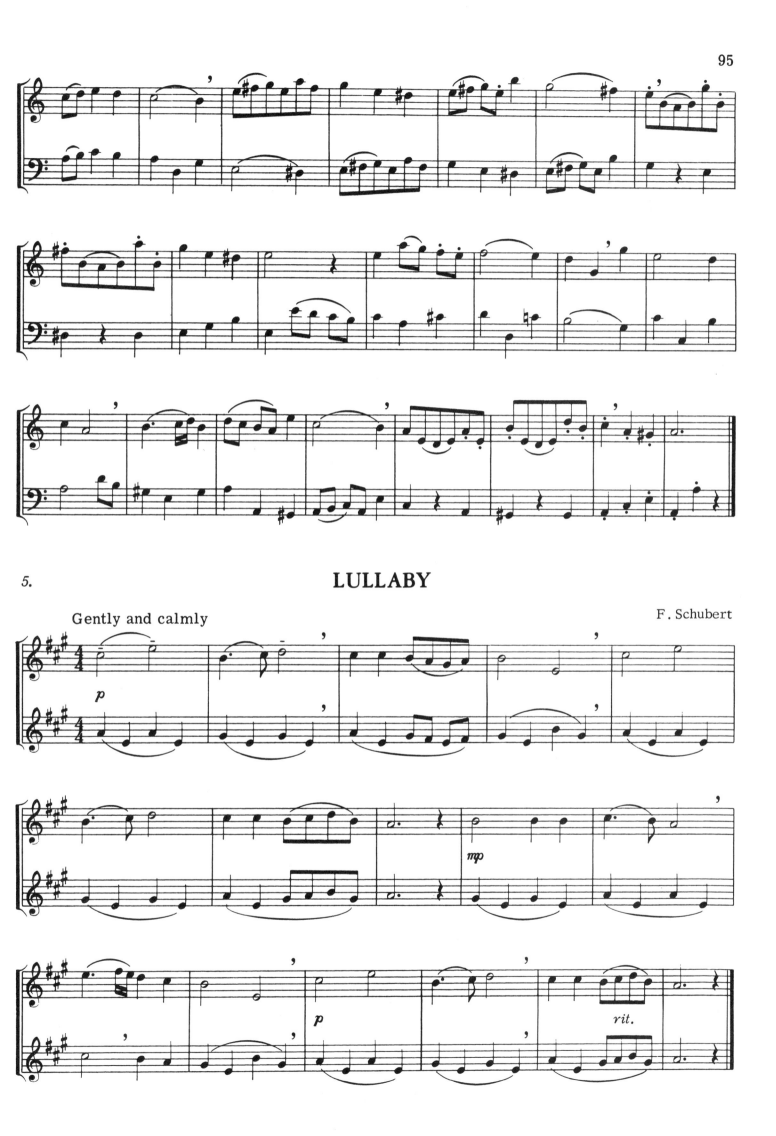

LULLABY

5.

F. Schubert

Gently and calmly

6.

ALLELUIA

W. A. Mozart

Brightly, with rich tone

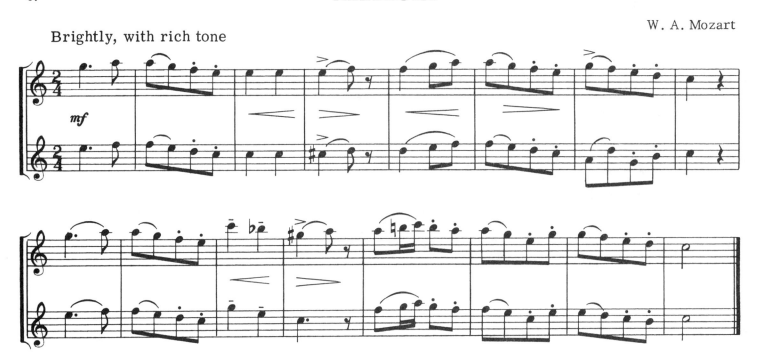

The following arrangement, specially made for two flutes, should be learned prior to playing the more familiar flute and piano version which has become part of every flute student's repertoire. Be most precise in your articulations. Come off the end notes of slurs marked thus: very lightly.

7. Gaily

TAMBOURIN

C. W. Gluck

ADDITIONAL MUSIC SUGGESTED FOR STUDY:

Solos: *Canzone*, by Classens (Editions Philippo, Paris)
          Tambourin, by Gluck-Barrère (Schirmer, N.Y.)
          Selected pieces from *La Flûte Classique*
          Gavotte from "Armide", by Gluck (A. Leduc, Paris)

Ensembles: *Duettino Pastorale*, by Avidom (Israel Music Inst., Tel Aviv)
           Menuetto from Trio II for three flutes, by Haydn (Schirmer, N.Y.)
           In the Realm of Dolls (4 fl.), by Maganini (Musicus, N.Y.)
           Village Festival, by S. Foster (Musicus, N.Y.)
           Rigaudon de Dardanus, by Rameau (Musicus, N.Y.)

LESSON IX
OTHER METRICAL UNITS

The eighth-note (♪) is frequently used as a metrical unit (in meter signatures, $\frac{4}{8}$, $\frac{6}{8}$) as is the sixteenth-note, although the latter ($\frac{4}{16}$, $\frac{3}{16}$) is less frequently found. The student is here given some simple exercises to accustom himself to the most common types of eighth-note rhythms and then is led to other slightly less common metrical values. A knowledge of various rhythms is valuable, especially in contemporary music.

RHYTHM EXERCISES

Beat or tap out each of these:

Less common rhythms which have been reintroduced by Bartok, Cowell, and other contemporary composers, as well as Oriental rhythms, include:

as well as more complicated combinations. More about this later.

Following are a number of familiar tunes in eighth-note rhythms.

1.

THE CAMPBELLS ARE COMING

Lively

THREE BLIND MICE

(Can be played as a 2- to 4-part round.)

UNDER THE GREENWOOD TREE

Th. A. Arne

GREENSLEEVES

Old English tune
(ca. 1600)

OLD FOLK MELODY

In the following lyrical solo, make each note *sing*.

LARGO from Sonata in G Minor

A. Vivaldi

Very slowly and smoothly

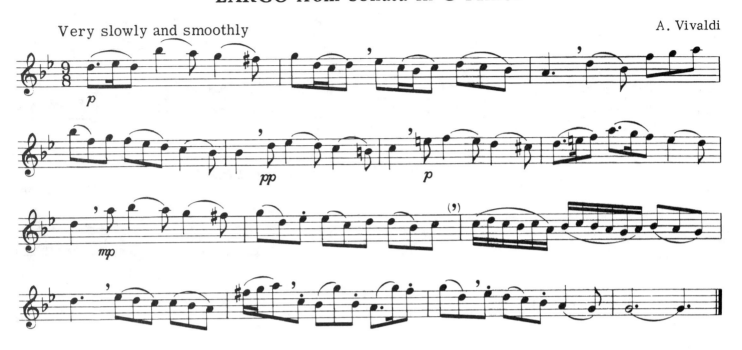

The next excerpt has an interesting problem for the student, as well as presenting him with a charming contemporary piece. After learning this section, buy the entire piece and learn it for a very attractive concert solo.

In the seventh bar, the parenthetical breath mark refers to the composer's original marking. However, a much more graceful and practical spot appears immediately following the next note, so we have indicated this as a preferable place at which to breathe. You will note that from that measure through the next five, no adequate breathing place is available. Preferably, the student should attempt to play the entire phrase without interrupting for breath. If, however, this is not possible at first, breathe after the highest note reached by the phrase (high D) so as to emphasize the climax tone.

SICILIENNE

M. Fusté-Lambezat

Andantino

Reprinted by permission of the Société des Editions Philippo, 24 Blvd. Poissonnière, Paris, 9.

The following extracts serve as examples of *style* (phrasing and articulation), *legato*, *wide interval study* (lip control), *melody* (tone), and *fluent fingering*.

THREE MOVEMENTS FROM A SUITE
I MENUET

C. Fischer

II BOURRÉE

III GIGUE

ECHO SONG from "Armide"

2 Flutes

C. W. Gluck

Allegretto

Write your own suggested tempo markings in the two following works. Also, add more dynamics if you feel the music needs this.

DANCE FOR TWO

SONG FOR TWO

after T. Benoit Berbiguier

DUO GRAZIOSO

after T. Benoit Berbiguier

RONDO

(Articulation Study)

L. Dorus

An additional way of presenting 3 in metrical units is by the use of a triplet, indicated

Thus, in $\frac{2}{4}$ meter, there is only this way of indicating "three-to-a-beat" instead of 2 or 4 or any multiple thereof.

Note that the *dotted note* is *longer*, and the *sixteenth note* is *shorter* in Example 2 than in any comparable notes in Example 1.

Beat this tricky little exercise:

Note the "slowed down" feeling by first having 4 to a beat, then 3, then 2, and finally 1.

Here are rhythmic examples to practice.

RHYTHMIC ETUDES

4.

5.

Frederick the Great

The triplet below introduces a flowing and smooth effect into other rhythms. In the small excerpt that follows, note how graceful an effect is created by the triplet in each phrase where it is used. It is advisable for the student to purchase the entire flute and piano part for performance.

SÉRÉNITÉ*

F. Passani

Andantino

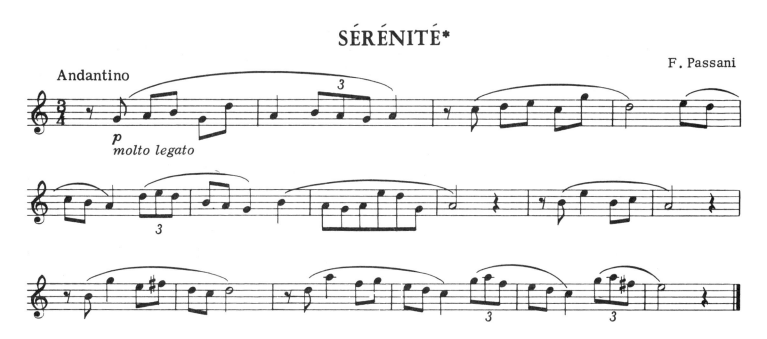

p
molto legato

* Reprinted by permission of the Société des Editions Philippo, 24 Blvd. Poissonnière, Paris, 9

MOVEMENT FOR FLUTE AND CELLO

G. F. Telemann

CHORD EXERCISES

The same exercise one half-step higher for the practice of sharps:

The same exercise can be played with these accidentals as well.

(Minor)  (all flatted)

The same chord exercise as a 4-note pattern in various keys.

Now, apply to the following all the rules you have learned.

PASTORALE

after L. Vinci

EXAMINATION II

Mark correct breathing places in 1 and 2, then play.

1.

2.

3: Play any two scales from memory.

4.

5. As fast as possible.

6. Flexible lip.

7. Watch meter signature changes.

ADDITIONAL MUSIC SUGGESTED FOR STUDY

Solos: Andante Cantabile, by M. Etgen (Editions Philippo, Paris)
Sicilienne, by Fusté-Lambezat (Editions Philippo)
Sérénité, by Passani (Editions Philippo)
Selected movements from Vivaldi Sonatas (McGinnis and Marx, N.Y.)
La Flûte Classique, Volumes I and II
Strolling, by M. Isaac (C. Fischer, N.Y.)

Ensemble: Sonata for two flutes and bass, by de la Barre (Pegasus, Locarno)

TO THE STUDENT

As you complete Volume I, you may wish to summarize what you have learned. Here are some basic rules which by now, we hope, have almost become habit. These will help you to practice well and to progress further on the road to becoming a good musician, for they teach you that *concentration* and *preparation* are two valuable keys to fun and pleasure in music:

1. Always practice new music slowly.

2. *Before playing a note,* check the meter signature, key signature, basic rhythms and accidentals.

3. *Then,* carefully look at articulations, register, dynamics.

4. Daily practice should include long tones and other exercises to develop a beautiful tone quality.

5. Daily practice should help you develop stamina and good breath control by doing push-ups and other exercises.

6. Do not lose the pleasure of accomplishment. Review the known or "old" music periodically. After all, music cannot all be new, and you may as well enjoy what you have worked hard to master.